My Precious
A Premature Baby Journal and N.I.C.U. report

ISBN - 13: 978-1978180703
ISBN - 10: 1978180705
Printed in the United States
First Edition: Sept. 2017

Disclaimer

This journal is a recording tool only to be used to deliver information. It is not meant to prevent, diagnose or recommend treatment for any illness or disease. Consult your Pediatrician, OBGYN, Neonatologist, or Family Physician for informed medical advice about your baby's health.

About this journal

Becoming the parents of a Preemie, and being a Preemie, can be a difficult journey. I created this journal to help you gather and keep your information about that experience organized. You can have a place to keep your medical information, N.I.C.U. records, pictures, phone numbers, resources and more, all in one place. It is a snapshot of this exciting time of your family's life.

To a Precious Warrior

Welcome to the world, Precious Warrior!
You have decided that it is time for your
grand entrance. You have a life to live,
things to learn and people to love. Your
journey here has been a challenge, but
you are a Warrior and you gave it your
all. You may have a few extra
challenges ahead of you, but you will
have much love and encouragement from
those around you to be able to face and
accomplish each one.

My first picture

About me

Name

Birthdate

Time I arrived

More about me

Weight _____

Length _____

Head Circumference _____

APGAR Score

Birthmarks

Who I look like

Hair Color

Blood Type

Condition at birth

In the beginning....
Mommy

In the beggining....

Daddy

Sonogram

My Baby Shower

Shower invitation

Come to our baby shower!

My Baby Shower

Where

Date   Time

Fun we had

Guests and Gifts

My Grand Entrance

Due Date/Arr. Date

When Mommy felt
I was coming

Where were we?

How we got to the hospital

How far was it?

What was the weather?

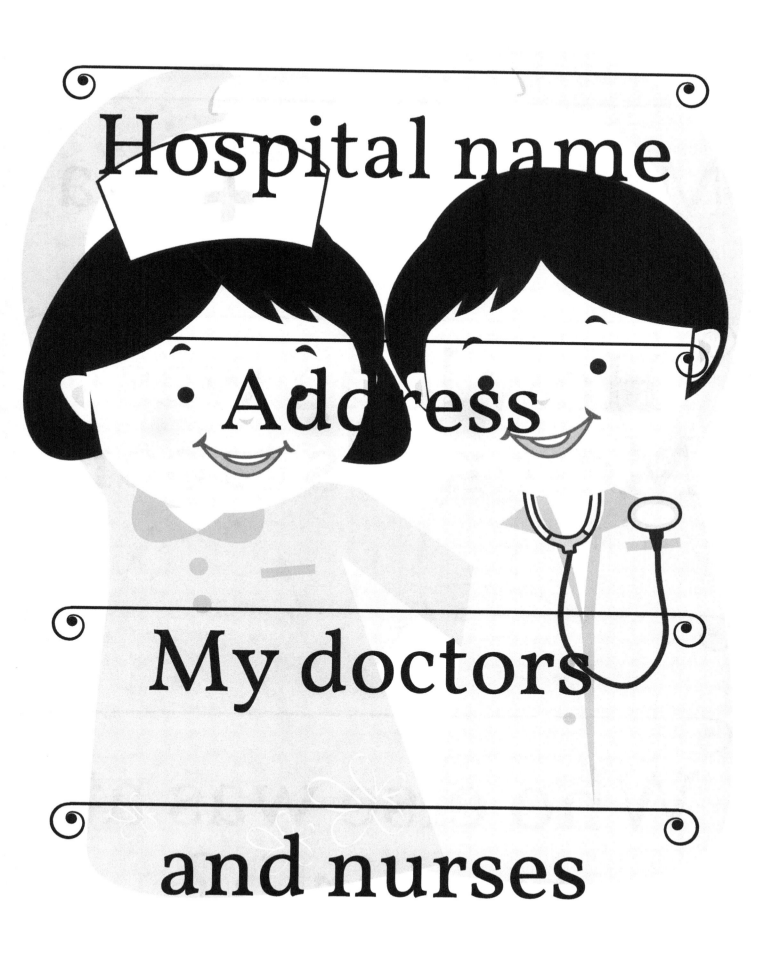

Midwife   Doula

How long was Mommy's labor

Who else was at my birth?

A letter to our baby

What was happening?

Who was president?

Popular songs/singers

Price of gas and diapers

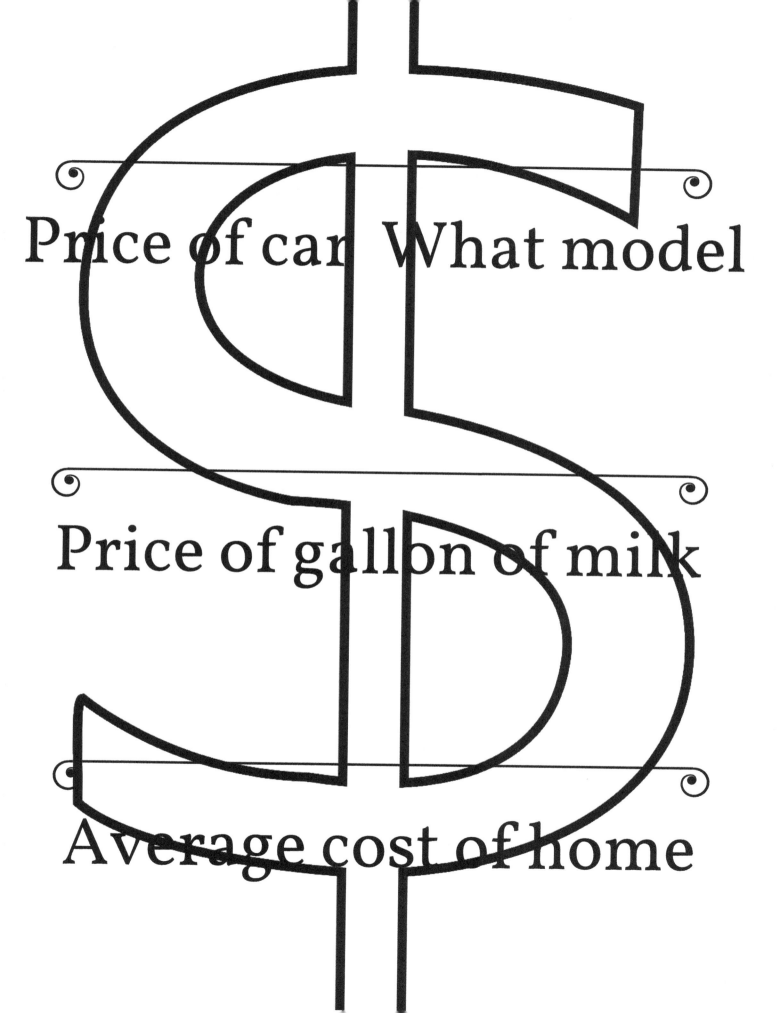

Price of car What model

Price of gallon of milk

Average cost of home

Fashion

Movies

Actresses

Actors

What the doctor said

Date	Comment

What the doctor said

Date	Comment

What the doctor said

Date   Comment

What the doctor said

Date	Comment

How we felt

Date	Notes

How we felt

Date	Notes

My family tree

Family Tree

My footprints

The N.I.C.U. Pictures

The N.I.C.U.

When I went in

Kind of isolette

Breathing support

The N.I.C.U.

What my parents did while keeping me company

First diaper change

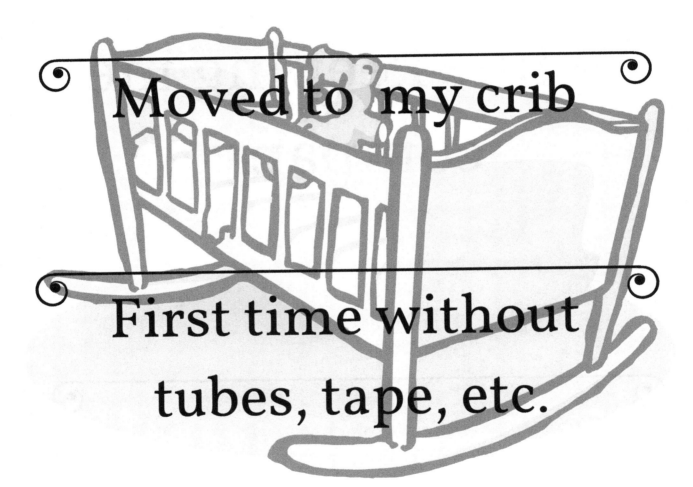

Moved to my crib

First time without tubes, tape, etc.

First bath

Milestones in the N.I.C.U.

First held by

First latched onto Mommy

First Kangaroo Care

These friends came to visit

My favorite toys to keep me company

N.I.C.U. Neighbors

Procedures etc.

X-Rays

Scans

Bilirubin

Jaundice

Other

Immunizations

Feeding

Feeding tube

I learned to suck

I learned to swallow

first gravage feeding

first bottle feeding

Respiration and sleep

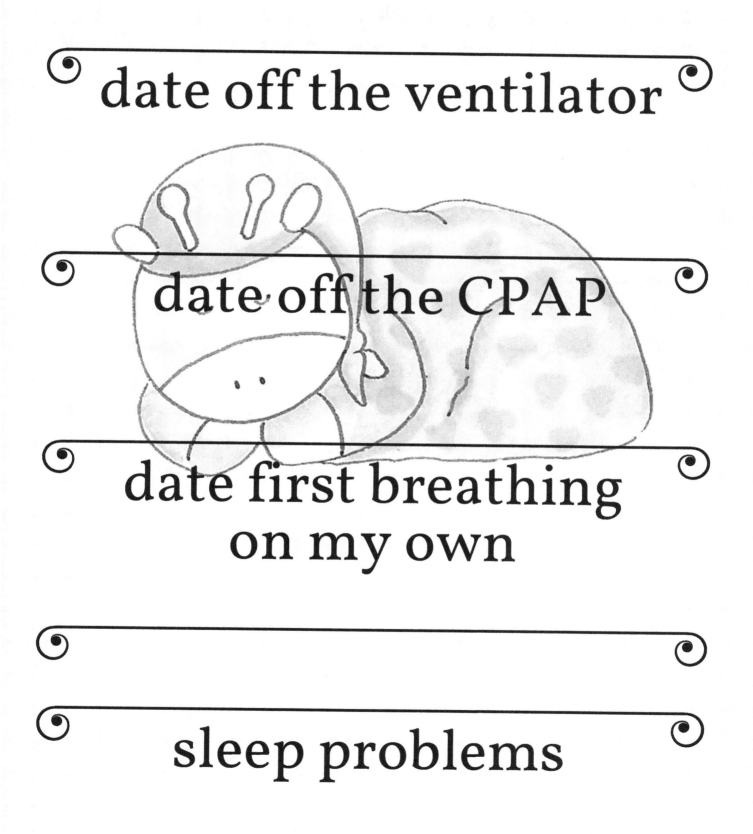

date off the ventilator

date off the CPAP

date first breathing
on my own

sleep problems

Pictures of us leaving the hospital

Before going home

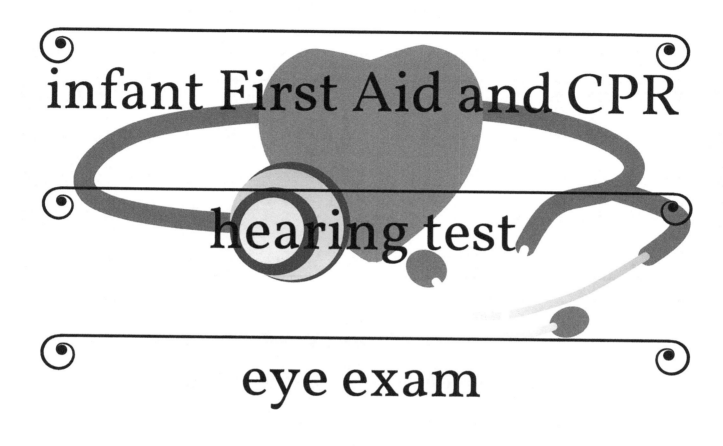

infant First Aid and CPR

hearing test

eye exam

apnea monitor training

preemie development evaluation

Coming home

Date

Age

Weight

Length

Picture of my room

How was my first day and night home

How did my family feel about my coming home

Date	Diaper change		Bath
	Pee	Poop	

Date Diaper change Bath

Pee   Poop

Date	Diaper change		Bath
	Pee	Poop	

Date	Diaper change		Bath
	Pee	Poop	

Date Diaper change Bath

Pee   Poop

Goals

Weekly height/Weight Head circumference

Date   Height   Weight   H/C

Weekly height/Weight Head circumference

Date	Height	Weight	H/C

Caregivers

Name	Ph. #	E-mail	Rate

Caregivers

Name	Ph. #	E-mail	Rate

Time to eat

Date	Time	oz/cc

Time to eat

Date	Time	oz/cc

Time to eat

Date	Time	oz/cc

Time to eat

Date	Time	oz/cc

Time to eat

Date	Time	oz/cc

Time to eat

Date	Time	oz/cc

Phone and Addresses

OBGYN

Hospital Receptionist

N.I.C.U. Desk

Lactation Counselor

Phone and Addresses

Social Worker

Emergency

N.I.C.U. Room

Misc.

Premature baby website links

Parents of Premature Babies
www.preemie-l.org

***

Prematurity.org

***

Tommy's CyberNursury

Preemie Web

***

grahamsfoundation.org

***

preemiestore.com

Premature baby website links

www.premature babies.co.uk

***

www.perfectlypreemie.com

***

www.babyprem.com

***

There are numerous Preemie stores on Etsy

Premature baby website links

www.americanpregnancy.
org/labor-and-birth/
premature-care/

***

www.miraclebabies.org.au/

***

www.babycenter.com/
premature-babies

Premature baby books

**Newborn Intensive Care:
What Every Parent Needs To Know**

Edited by Jeanette Zaichkin

***

**Parenting Your Premature Baby
and Child: The Emotional Journey**

Debra L. Davis   Mara Tesler Stein

***

**The Preemie Parents' Companion:
The Essential Guide for Taking
Care of Your Baby in the Hospital,
at Home and Through the
First Years**

Susan L. Madden

Your Premature Baby and Child: Helpful Answers and Advice from Parents

Amy E. Tracy   Dianne I. Moroney

***

Preemies: The Essential Guide to Premature Babies

Dana Weschler Linden

Emma Trenti Paeoli

Mia Weschler Doran M.D.

***

Your Premature Baby: The First 5 Years

Nikki Bradford

The Premature Baby Book:
A Parents Guide to Coping and Caring in the First Five Years

Helen Harrison   Anne Kositski

***

Pediatric Massage: For the Child with Special Needs

Kathy Drehob   Mary Gengler Fuhr

***

Your Premature Baby: Everything You Need to Know About Childbirth, Treatment and Parenting

Frank G. Manginello

Theresa Foy Digeronimo

Breastfeeding Your Premature Baby
by Gwen Gotsch

***

The N.I.C.U. Rollercoaster
by Nichole E. Zimmerman
Edward J. Sprague

***

Alex: The Fathering of a Preemie
Jeff Stimpson

Coming To Term: A Father's Story of Birth, Loss and Survival
William H. Jr. Woodwell

***

Born Too Soon
Elizabeth Mehren

***

You Are Not Alone: The N.I.C.U. Experience
Children's Medical Ventures

Kangaroo Care: The Best You Can Do to Help Your Pre-term Infant

Susan Lungington-Hoe

***

What to Do When Your Baby is Premature: A Parents Handbook for Coping With High-Risk Pregnancy and Caring for the Preterm Infant

Sharon Simmons Hornfischer

Kangaroo Care

Kangaroo Care is the practice of holding a baby wearing just a diaper in an upright position against the parent's chest. It is also called skin-to-skin care. The baby can be secured with a stretchy wrap or be placed inside the adult's shirt and/or have a receiving blanket placed across her back. It is practiced to provide developmental care to premature babies for 6 months and full-term babies for 3 months.

Kangaroo Care benefits to your baby:

improve breastfeeding

reduce death

reduce hospital infection

stabilize the baby's heart rate

improve breathing patterns

imp. oxygen saturation levels

gain in sleep time

decrease crying

earlier hospital discharge

Kangaroo Care benefits to parents:

improved bonding and feelings of closeness with their babies

increased breast milk supply

increased confidence in the ability to care for their babies

increased confidence that their babies are well cared for

increased sense of control

Kangaroo Care Websites

https://my.clevelandclinic.org/
health/articles/skin-to-skin-
contact-for-you-and-your-baby

***

https://my.clevelandclinic.org/
health/articles/premature-labor

***

kangaroomothercare.com

***

www.bliss.org.uk/skin-to-skin-
and-kangaroo-care

When I am Stressed I Can :

read a book   *   get a massage

draw * do yoga * exercise

go for a walk * listen to music

talk to a friend * plan a garden

watch a funny movie

meditate * nap * laugh

deep breathing exercises

write a story * ride my bike

write thank-you notes

Hopefully, you will be able to disregard this section. If your baby has indeed passed, my wish is that this information will help bring you some comfort and support. The purpose for the following section is to assist you in remembering an angel that has graced your lives.

Websites for Support

www.marchforbabies.org

***

www.whattoexpect.com/
pregnancy/emotional-
life/grief-and-loss/losing-
a-premature-baby.aspx

www.lifescript/Health.com

***

www.lullabyetrust.org.uk/
bereavement-support/

***

www.verywell.com/
coping-with-neonatal-
death-or-loss-of-a-
premature-baby-237177

Notes

Notes

Notes

Notes

Made in the USA
Monee, IL
04 November 2019